CHEMICAL DEPENDENCY AND THE DYSFUNCTIONAL FAMILY

Many young people feel that they have no one to help them deal with their problems with drugs and alcohol.

THE DRUG ABUSE PREVENTION LIBRARY

CHEMICAL DEPENDENCY AND THE DYSFUNCTIONAL FAMILY

Jeff Biggers

THE ROSEN PUBLISHING GROUP, INC.
NEW YORK

Published in 1998 by The Rosen Publishing Group, Inc.
29 East 21st Street, New York, NY 10010

Copyright © 1998 by The Rosen Publishing Group, Inc.

Library of Congress Cataloging-in-Publication Data

Biggers, Jeff.
    Chemical dependency and the dysfunctional family / Jeff Biggers.
    p. cm. — (The drug abuse prevention library)
    Includes bibliographical references and index.
    Summary: Discusses the causes and dangers of chemical dependency, its effects on the family, and ways to get help in dealing with this problem.
    ISBN 0-8239-2749-0 (lib. bdg.)
    1. Drug abuse—United States—Juvenile literature. 2. Alcoholism—United States—Juvenile literature. 3. Problem families—United States—Juvenile literature. 4. Children of narcotic addicts—United States—Juvenile literature. 5. Children of alcoholics—United States—Juvenile literature. [1. Drug abuse. 2. Alcoholism.] I. Title. II. Series.
HV5809.5.B54 1998
362.29'13'0973—dc21   98-20873
                                              CIP
                                              AC

Manufactured in the United States of America

Contents

Introduction

Shaneen is tired of baby-sitting her two younger sisters. At age sixteen, it's the last thing she wants to do on a Friday night. Shaneen's mother left a message on the refrigerator saying that she would be back before dinner. It's already eight o'clock. Shaneen knows that her mother, who has a new boyfriend, won't make it back until at least midnight. When she does, Shaneen's mom won't be sober.

Mark, her brother, is rarely home. He likes to hang out with his friends, who have their own apartments. Shaneen hardly ever sees her father. He lives thirty miles away with his new family. He doesn't have time to visit anymore.

Shaneen is missing out on a great party tonight. Everyone else is there. They have two kegs, so there will be plenty to drink.

*Shaneen looks at the clock. It's almost ten. | 7
She can't wait much longer. She needs a drink.*

*Seventeen-year-old Ray left his house a few
hours ago already stoned. His parents are at a
business party. He's glad that they left him plenty
of spending money. They always do, especially
since they have so many meetings to attend. With
the spending money they left him, Ray will be able
to buy enough drugs for the coming weekend.
Ray knows that he isn't totally on his own.
According to his mother, he gets so unhappy
because he is going through a difficult phase. She
says that it's natural for someone his age. "He
doesn't talk to me," she tells her friends. That's
how she explains why they never spend time
together. Ray's mom gets mad at him if he brings
home poor grades or doesn't clean his room. He
knows that his mother is concerned about what
other people think. She wants her friends and co-
workers to know that everything is going well. In
Ray's family, nothing but success is acceptable.
Ray's father, on the other hand, just laughs at
Ray's behavior most of the time. Once he came
home early on a Friday night and found Ray
stoned. At first his dad seemed very angry. But
his anger didn't last long. Later he laughed and
said that Ray reminded him of himself in his
youth. "I was always getting into trouble, too," he
said, and smiled.*

8 | *Two Families*

Shaneen's lifestyle is not unusual, nor is Ray's. Today, at school or at home, thousands of teenagers are looking for a fix. For some, it's just a matter of getting another drink of alcohol. Others are hooked on the street drugs that Ray prefers, such as cocaine, crack, or heroin. Some are abusing prescription drugs, such as Valium, Ritalin, or Percodan.

Many teens abuse drugs. Some use them every day. These teens are not drinking or using drugs to relax, to wind down, or to get high anymore. They use drugs because they are chemically dependent, or addicted to drugs. This means that they have a physical and/or psychological dependence on drugs. If they do not use the drugs, they will experience painful withdrawal symptoms.

Withdrawal is the physical or psychological process that your body goes through when you are coming down from drugs. There are many symptoms, including confusion, sweating, shaking, and feeling hot, cold, or extreme pain.

Dysfunctional families and chemical dependency often go hand in hand. Sometimes a functional family can become dysfunctional because of chemical dependency. For example, Shaneen's family was happier and more peaceful before her 9 mother started drinking. Her mother's alcoholism led to dysfunction in the family. It contributed to problems such as divorce, neglect, emotional abuse, and, finally, Shaneen's own alcohol abuse.

In other cases, living in a dysfunctional family leads to chemical dependency. Ray has turned to chemicals to deal with his parents' emotional neglect and workaholic lifestyle. In Ray's case, the chemical dependency has not caused the family's dysfunction; it is the result of it.

For Shaneen and Ray, and for everyone else, it is not too late to get help. Unfortunately, teens in dysfunctional families often cannot get assistance from their parents. Part of the problem is that they have to face chemical dependency on their own.

Today every teenager is confronted by the pressure to use alcohol and drugs. Many young people are on their own when it comes to handling problems. Like Shaneen and Ray, a lot of teens have no one in their families they believe they can count on. Their families have let them down. They may be embarrassed to speak to a friend or teacher. But here's the truth: they aren't alone. With or without their families' help, teens can conquer chemical dependency.

Every teenager today faces pressure from his or her peers to use drugs or alcohol.

CHAPTER 1

Chemicals Are in Control

You may have heard the terms "drug abuse," "chemical dependency," and "drug addiction." But do you really understand what they mean?

Drug abuse is the abuse of all drugs, including alcohol. However, some people separate drugs and alcohol. These people may use the term "substance abuse" to show that they are talking about all drugs, including alcohol. No matter what you call it, drug abuse means that your drug or alcohol use causes you to act in a way that hurts yourself and others.

Both chemical dependency and drug addiction describe the point at which a person has developed a tolerance to a drug. Tolerance is when you need more and more

12 | of a drug to get the same effect (or high) that you once got from smaller amounts. Someone who is chemically dependent, or addicted to a drug, also needs to use the drug to keep from going through withdrawal. Alcoholism is the term used to describe an addiction to alcohol.

Before you can understand chemical dependency, you need to learn about chemicals and the effects drugs have on your mind and body.

Drugs and Chemical Dependency
The U.S. government organizes all illegal drugs into five categories, called schedules.

Schedule I
Schedule I includes drugs that are very addictive and have no medical use in the United States. They include heroin, a narcotic that can be injected, sniffed, or smoked; both marijuana and hashish, which are from the cannabis plant and can be smoked or eaten; and LSD, a hallucinogen that can be eaten.

Schedule II
Schedule II drugs are very addictive, but can be used for medical purposes if their use is strictly controlled by a doctor.

Schedule II drugs include opium, a narcotic that can be eaten or smoked; morphine, a narcotic that can be eaten, smoked, or injected; cocaine, which includes crack and is a stimulant that can be sniffed, smoked, or injected; amphetamines, a stimulant that can be eaten or injected; and phencyclidine, also called PCP, which is a hallucinogen that can be smoked, eaten, or injected.

Schedules III, IV, V

Schedule III, IV, and V drugs are not as addictive as Schedule I and II drugs. However, they are still dangerous. Their use should be monitored closely by a doctor. Doctors often prescribe Schedule III, IV, and V drugs as medication for coughing, vomiting, diarrhea, and weight control. They include Valium, Librium, some forms of codeine, and many others.

All drugs can be addictive, even prescription drugs. However, Schedule I and II drugs pose the most danger. Anyone taking them has a high risk of developing a severe chemical dependency.

Alcohol is not classified since it is a legal, non-prescription drug. However, it is severely addictive. Many alcohol abusers become chemically dependent on alcohol.

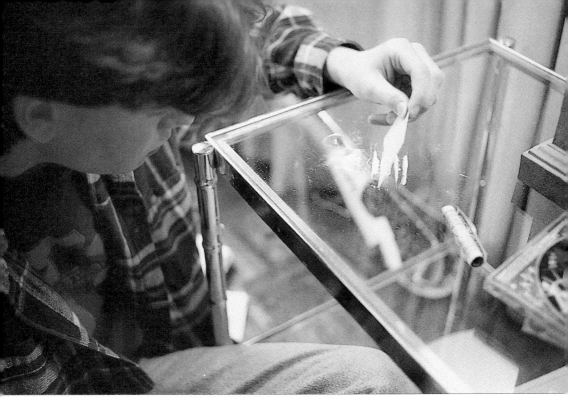

Cocaine, a Schedule II drug, is very addictive.

How Does Chemical Dependency Occur?

Most people go through similar stages that lead to chemical dependency. Not everyone has the same experiences, but these are the most common. Chemical dependency is a process. It happens at different rates depending upon the drug and the person who is taking it.

1. First, you experiment with drugs. People first take drugs for many different reasons. You may try drugs because of pressures at home, coaxing from friends, or curiosity about how a drug will make you feel.

2. Your tolerance increases. The more chemicals you use, the more drugs you need to get the same effect.

3. You may have blackouts. There may be times when you do not remember what you did when you were drinking or taking drugs.

4. You avoid talking about drugs or alcohol. As your addiction develops, you try to take attention away from anything that will point it out.

5. You become preoccupied with drug use. You spend time thinking about drugs, plan your use carefully, and choose your friends based on drugs.

6. You blame others and make excuses for your drug use. You may even cause fights as an excuse to drink. This stage is called denial.

7. You lose control of your drug use. You cannot control how much you use or stop yourself from taking more drugs. You may feel weak or think that you do not have willpower.

8. Your drug use affects your family, friends, or education. Drugs may destroy your relationships. You may skip school to take drugs.

9. You may have medical, legal, or psychiatric problems. Chemical dependency brings many difficulties.

10. You lose hope. As your addiction gets worse, you may feel as though there is nothing you can do to stop it. You may feel as if your life has lost its meaning or is not worth living.

Long-Term Effects of Chemical Dependency
Chemical dependency, or drug addiction, can have very serious consequences.

Stimulants
Some drugs are called stimulants. These drugs, like cocaine and amphetamines, make you feel powerful or alert. Some people refer to them as uppers. Stimulants include cocaine, crack, amphetamines, and prescription drugs such as Benzedrine and Sanorex. Stimulants increase your blood pressure, pulse rate, and energy level. They can cause you to feel excited. They produce insomnia, paranoia, and hallucinations.

The U.S. government classifies all illegal drugs into five categories, called schedules.

Long-term consequences can include weight loss, anxiety, severe depression, violent behavior, heart failure, and suicide. Cocaine and crack also can damage the inside of the nose and cause other serious problems.

Depressants

Some drugs are called depressants. These drugs, such as alcohol and sleeping pills, can make you feel tired, indifferent, or sad. Some people call them downers. These include alcohol, barbiturates, and prescription drugs, such as tranquilizers and Valium. Depressants slow down bodily functions. Dizziness, nausea, headaches, convulsions, and memory loss can follow an initial sense of pleasure.

18 Over a long period of time, depression, fatigue, insomnia, respiratory failure, psychotic episodes (losing contact with reality completely), and suicide can occur. Alcohol also can cause blackouts, memory loss, weight gain, and cirrhosis of the liver.

Narcotics

Narcotics, also called opiates, include codeine, heroin, methadone, morphine, and prescription pain pills such as Percodan. They relieve pain. You may feel sleepy, relaxed, and extremely happy. But your pain does not go away forever. It simply is postponed. Narcotics are some of the most addictive drugs.

They can increase your risk of contracting HIV if you share needles. They can also cause heart and breathing problems, mood swings, and tremors.

Hallucinogens

Hallucinogens include marijuana and hashish, both from the cannabis plant. They make you feel relaxed. Large doses might cause agitation or excitement. Other hallucinogens, such as LSD and magic mushrooms, change your thinking and your perception of reality. You may hallucinate—see or feel things that aren't there. Hallucinogens impair judgment and coordination, putting you at risk for self-injury.

Long-term consequences, including violent behavior, paranoia, depression, and flashbacks, may occur. Marijuana also may cause low sperm count in men, infertility in women, and weight gain.

Inhalants

Inhalants are drugs such as nitrous oxide, called laughing gas. Many common products, such as hair spray, nail polish remover, glue, paint, and gasoline, produce fumes that are inhaled and can be abused. Taking inhalants may slur your speech, impair your coordination, and cause you to feel drunk. They can slow your breathing and cause nausea and vomiting.

Over a long period of time, use can lead to brain damage, severe depression, nerve damage, suffocation, and sudden death.

Chemical dependency has severe consequences for your body, brain, and relationships with other people. What starts out as a careless experiment with drugs can begin a long journey toward drug addiction. For some people, that journey ends in disease or even death. That's why it is important to get help before it is too late.

CHAPTER 2

Dysfunctional Families

Shaneen was used to picking up after her mother. She constantly cleaned up after her mother's drinking, accidents, and embarrassing behavior when she was drunk. Shaneen had to take over all the household chores because her mother couldn't do them. Shaneen knew life wasn't supposed to be this way, but she didn't know what to do.

Shaneen's mom was rarely home. When she was, she was drunk. Shaneen's home was filled with disorder, confusion, and pain. There was a huge hole in Shaneen's life: her family was missing. Shaneen wanted to escape from it all.

From the outside Ray's family looked completely different from Shaneen's. They seemed to be the perfect family. They had a lot of money, a big house, and expensive cars.

Money was never a problem in Ray's house. *However, his parents' jobs demanded a lot of time. Ray's brother said he didn't mind. He was in college and was at class or with friends most of the time. Ray, though, was always waiting around for his mom and dad.*

Ray's parents knew that something was wrong. They suspected he might be using drugs. He's a smart boy, his parents thought. He knows what's right and what's wrong. They were both too busy to worry about Ray.

Finally, Ray decided that his family didn't matter anymore. Like Shaneen, he had a huge hole in his life. Drugs were there to fill the gap.

In a sense, Shaneen and Ray are emotional orphans. Their parents are consumed by things such as their jobs, their friends, or their drug abuse. Their parents have not been supportive as role models, teachers, or positive influences.

Every family has problems, and every family goes through difficult times. No family is perfect, and no one should feel bad because his or her family is going through a rough period. The difference between occasional spats, disagreements, and even turmoil and real dysfunctional behavior is that dysfunctional behavior

22 has more serious and long-lasting consequences. Dysfunctional families can't rebound. They cannot forgive and go on. They drift further apart. They may be on the verge of having a complete breakdown.

What Families Need

In order for a family to be functional, family members' needs must be met. All families cannot meet all these needs all of the time. This does not mean that your family is dysfunctional. However, if your family cannot fulfill many of the needs, or cannot fulfill them a majority of the time, then you may need help.

Survival

Families need to provide each other with life's basic necessities. These include food, shelter, clothing, and health care.

Safety and Security

Family members should feel safe physically and emotionally in a family. Parents have a responsibility to protect their children from abuse—physical, sexual, and emotional.

Love and Belonging

Family members need to feel loved. They should know they are welcomed and valued.

Every member of a family needs to feel secure in order to grow.

Self-Esteem
Having self-esteem means that you realize that you are an important, capable, worth-while person. A family that values, supports, and encourages each member meets its need for self-esteem.

Growth
Everyone has to grow and change throughout his or her lifetime. A family that nurtures its members with love, respect, and open communication helps its members to grow emotionally.

Skills for Independent Living
There is a lot to learn before someone can live independently. Family members need

24 to learn how to solve problems and to make decisions wisely.

What Is a Dysfunctional Family?

Dysfunctional means something that does not work. A dysfunctional family is a family that does not meet the needs of its members. Many things can cause a family to be dysfunctional. A dysfunctional family might not support or show love for its members. It may not provide any emotional care—it might be full of threats, insults, physical violence, and tremendous conflict. Members may neglect each other. Parents may be unable or unwilling to be part of their children's lives physically or emotionally. They may abuse each other physically, emotionally, or sexually.

In dysfunctional families, young people often are solely responsible for themselves. They may find themselves making decisions about everything from schoolwork to friends and jobs. As you get older, you must make your own decisions. But teens in dysfunctional families have not been taught how to make smart choices. Instead, they must figure things out for themselves.

These teens often do not have role models or a sense of order in their lives. Teens in dysfunctional families have to face the world on their own.

What is a dysfunctional family? How do I know if my family is functioning "normally"?

Many teens living in dysfunctional families turn to alcohol or drugs for relief. These teens use drugs or alcohol to dull their pain and to cope with their chaotic lives. They do not see any other way to escape their families, and no one in their families is around to help them. In a dysfunctional family, the other family members often are so wrapped up in their own problems that they do not notice the teen's drug abuse. The abuse gets worse and worse until the teen becomes chemically dependent.

A Scale of Dysfunction

Almost no family is entirely functional or dysfunctional, just as no person is all good or all bad. Most families fall somewhere in

26 | the middle of the scale. Remember, every family has problems. Dysfunctional families usually have more problems, bigger problems, and harder problems to solve.

Obvious Dysfunction

Shaneen's family is an example of obvious dysfunction. Although Shaneen tries to hide her family's problems, it is not hard to tell that something is seriously wrong.

Shaneen's family is experiencing several types of dysfunction. First, Shaneen's mother is an alcoholic. She puts her need for alcohol before the needs of her children. Her mother also is emotionally abusive. She argues with her children constantly and blames them for her drinking problem. Finally, she is neglectful. She cannot carry out all of her responsibilities as a parent. Shaneen's mother neglects her children's needs, leaving Shaneen to make up for her absence and responsibilities.

In a seriously dysfunctional family, very few of the members' needs are being met. Shaneen's family is surviving, but barely. No one feels safe or secure in the family. Fights break out suddenly. The best way for the children to protect themselves is to stay out of their mother's way.

There also is very little love in Shaneen's home. No one feels as though he or she belongs. All members are on their own. Their self-esteem is very low. They all know that they are not as important to their mother as the alcohol is.

Shaneen's family has very serious problems. They are struggling with several dysfunctions. Their needs are not being met. Shaneen's family worries about the most basic things, such as food, shelter, and safety. They are too busy trying to survive to be concerned about growth, communication, and skills for independent living.

Subtle Dysfunction

The problems in Ray's family are more subtle. The family is dysfunctional in several ways. His parents are workaholics. They have made their careers more important than their family. They also are neglectful because they are emotionally distant. Although Ray's parents give him necessities, such as food, clothing, and shelter, they do not give him love, interest, protection, or time.

Like Shaneen, Ray has a family that is not meeting its members' needs. Fortunately, Ray has everything necessary for survival, safety, and security. However, because his parents no longer participate actively in his

A codependent teenager may cover up an addict's behavior, accidents, or neglect.

life, Ray does not feel as though he belongs
in the family. He is not getting the love he
needs from them. As a result, his family is
not meeting his need for love and belonging.

Also, Ray is not able to change or to grow.
His parents do not support him or encourage him to try new things or to improve
himself. Because the family members do not
communicate with each other, they are
stuck repeating the same old dysfunctional
behaviors.

Finally, Ray is not learning how to live
independently, since his parents are never
there to teach him. They simply leave him
alone and instead expect him to take care
of himself.

The dysfunction in Ray's family might
not be as serious as it is in Shaneen's, but
it does exist. Ray can no longer count on
his family to function on his behalf. His
family structure—which is supposed to
support him, teach him, and come to his
rescue—has completely fallen to pieces.
Ray is on his own, too.

The unhealthy patterns in Ray's family
have led him to use drugs as an escape.
Using drugs to cope with a dysfunctional
family is discussed in Chapter 4. But first,
it is useful to explore another side of chemical dependency: codependency.

CHAPTER 3

Codependency

*S*haneen, Ray, and their families are codependent. Codependency is a pattern of behavior that results in unhealthy relationships. It may mean that there is an unequal amount of give-and-take in a relationship, or that there is a lack of clear personal boundaries (limits) between two or more people.

Caring Codependents

Codependency is found in many troubled and stressful families. It occurs in all kinds of dysfunctional families, especially in families with addicted loved ones. In these families, the codependents are the people who enable loved ones to continue their addiction to drugs or alcohol. Usually

spouses, siblings, parents, and children

are codependents. Other family members and friends often are codependents, too.

These codependents have very good intentions. They are trying to cope with the chemical dependency of someone they love very much. Often it seems best to make up excuses or stories to protect the alcoholic or addict. Codependents cover the accidents and chaos left by people who are chemically dependent. They have learned that this behavior helps their day-to-day survival. Also, they often cannot deal with all the emotions that the chemical dependency or other dysfunction causes: shame, guilt, anger, fear, hatred, and others.

Poor Behavioral Patterns

At the root of codependency are patterns of behavior that create unhealthy relationships. Codependents often feel as though they need to take care of other people. In doing so, they ignore their own needs. They act as "caretakers." This means that they care for someone else by doing things that the person actually could do on his or her own. They also act as "rescuers" when they try to save someone from the results of his or her own poor behavior.

A codependent may believe that the only way he or she can be happy is by making others happy.

Many codependents have low self-esteem. They believe that they can be liked by others if they take care of them. To feel good about themselves, they have to be able to solve problems for others. However, no one can solve all of someone else's problems. When codependents fail, they feel lonely, depressed, and worthless.

Are You Codependent?
Not all codependents look alike. However, if you answer "yes" to many of the following statements, you may want to take a closer look at your behavior.

- I am afraid no one will like me;
- I try to avoid conflict as much as possible;
- Other people's happiness is more important than my own;
- When things go wrong, it's my fault;
- People do not really like me. They are just pretending;
- I never do anything right.

Codependents think they are helping someone they love. By keeping the dysfunction a secret, they believe they are making things more peaceful and easier for everyone in the family.

34 | *Hiding the Addiction*

Shaneen has been her mother's codependent for years. She avoids arguments at all costs. Shaneen stays away from her mother when she is drunk. She cleans up her mother's messes and takes care of her sisters. She makes excuses to the bill collectors when there is no money and to her mother's co-workers when her mother is too hung over to go to work. Shaneen has kept her family's problems a secret while sinking deeper into her own despair.

Codependents like Shaneen often do not see a way to get help for the alcoholic or drug addict. To them, admitting the problem exists would be abandoning or betraying someone they love. For Shaneen, the only way to escape her problems is through alcohol.

There are better ways for Shaneen to cope with her mother's chemical dependency. She does not have to be a codependent. She also does not have to turn to alcohol to dull her pain.

Shaneen first has to learn to take care of herself. She has to focus on her own life, not her mother's. A big part of this change is acknowledging her buried feelings. Before Shaneen can move on, she has to recognize that she is angry at her mother

for drinking. She also has to acknowledge | *35*
that she feels emotions such as guilt, fear,
and shame about her family.

Then Shaneen needs to learn to communicate. She must realize that making
excuses and lying do not help. Eventually
she will be able to express her concerns to
her mother. First, however, she can practice
talking about her feelings and letting them
out. Shaneen can turn to a trusted friend, a
teacher, a guidance counselor, or another
adult who cares about her. When she is
ready to talk to her mother, this support
person can be there too.

By taking control of her life, Shaneen is
helping herself. She is taking control and
no longer being a codependent.

Ignoring the Addiction

In Ray's family, codependency appears in
another way. Ray's father has refused to
look closely at his son's problems. Instead,
he thinks that he is being a protective and
understanding parent.

Ray's mother has ignored her son's drug
addiction for the sake of family stability. To
mention it out loud would create conflict
and turmoil in the family. It is easier for her
to pretend the chemical dependency does
not exist. In reality, the addiction keeps

36 getting worse. Codependents often think that by not talking about a drug addiction, it will heal itself and vanish.

At first, it seems as if Ray's family might be able to keep up this act. But a tremendous amount of resentment and pain remains inside the family, behind all of the cover-ups, excuses, and lies. His family members believe they are helping him by covering up his chemical dependency. However, the conflict does not go away. It just boils beneath the surface.

Ray's parents need to acknowledge their son's drug problem and recognize the feelings that the addiction causes in them. Then Ray's parents have to learn to communicate with their son again. They may not be able to do this alone. A drug counselor can work with the entire family to end the codependent behavior and help Ray.

Ray and Shaneen's families are both dysfunctional and codependent. Both families have serious problems. Worse, they have learned unhealthy and harmful ways of dealing with their problems: they are codependent. Fortunately, behaviors that are learned also can be unlearned.

CHAPTER 4

Using Drugs to Cope with Your Family

*T*eens turn to drugs for many different reasons. Some cannot deal with the dysfunction in their families. Others are the children of alcoholics or drug addicts. These teens are at an even higher risk of chemical dependency than most people. Finally, some give in to peer pressure to take drugs or drink alcohol. Many of these young people do not have role models or trusted adults they can turn to for advice.

Pressures at Home
Many teens have serious family problems. Sometimes drugs and alcohol seem to be the only way to cope with family life.

Physical Abuse
Parents, stepparents, siblings, and other family members can be abusers. Physical

38 abuse occurs when someone touches you in a way that causes pain or physical harm.

Emotional Abuse

Emotional abuse occurs when someone's words or actions damage your self-esteem. Emotional abusers may bully you, call you names, or purposely embarrass you.

Sexual Abuse

Sexual abuse consists of uncomfortable sexual contact or behavior. It may be as violent as rape or as seemingly nonviolent as viewing pornographic movies.

Drug Abuse

Drug abuse by a family member can result in a dysfunctional family. It can lead to everything from codependency to physical abuse to a loss of family income.

Neglect

Parents who fail to provide life's basic necessities are guilty of neglect. These needs include food, water, shelter, clothing, and health care. If a family is unable to afford these things, it is the parent's responsibility to seek help to get them.

Workaholic Parent

Today the majority of parents work outside the home. Most working parents can balance their careers and their families

Parents who place more importance on their careers than on their children or their families are called workaholics.

successfully. However, when a parent's career takes priority over his or her children or family, he or she is called a workaholic.

Depression or Other Mental Illness
Many teens struggle with mental illness such as depression and anxiety. Others do not experience full-blown mental illness, but still feel unhappy, anxious, or lonely.

Children of Alcoholics

Children of alcoholics and drug addicts are at special risk to develop chemical dependency. There is strong scientific evidence that alcoholism tends to run in families. Children of alcoholics are three to four times more likely to become alcoholics than **39**

It can be difficult to ignore pressure to use drugs or alcohol if you do not have a family that will encourage you to say no.

children of non-alcoholics. Studies show that 13 to 25 percent of all children of alcoholics are likely to become alcoholics.

Alcoholism may run in families for several reasons. First, scientific research shows that there may be a genetic predisposition to alcoholism. Having a genetic predisposition means that you have a higher risk of becoming an alcoholic than other people because of your genes. Genes are passed from parents to children. So if your parent is an alcoholic, you may have inherited genes that make you more susceptible to alcoholism.

Also, alcoholic parents pass on their behavior to their children. Children learn to do many things by watching their *41* parents. They might learn to paint, to wash dishes, or to drive a car. Or they might learn to cope. When a daughter sees her mother coping with problems by drinking, she may be tempted to try it herself.

Children of Drug Addicts

Chemical dependency in the children of drug addicts has not been very widely studied. Scientists do not know if a genetic link exists. However, teens whose parents are drug addicts are at a higher risk for chemical dependency. Drugs may be an accepted part of their upbringing. They may simply be presented as a part of life. To these teens, drugs are familiar. They have watched their family members use and abuse drugs. When things get tough, they may try it themselves.

Peer Pressure

Drugs and alcohol tempt all teens at some time. Most young people today either have tried some form of drug or know someone who has. Many have seen their friends, their brothers and sisters, and even their parents doing drugs or abusing alcohol.

"Everybody's Doing It"

Why do people start using drugs or alcohol? Many young people drink or take drugs to impress their friends. They may be experiencing a lot of peer pressure. Peer pressure is when your friends or your peers try to push you to do something you're not sure you want to do. Everyone feels peer pressure in his or her life. Everyone wants to fit in, be accepted, and be considered important. These feelings are normal and natural. But some people try to take advantage of other people's need for approval by convincing them to do things that are bad for them.

Peer pressure is hard to ignore, especially when you do not have a family to depend on. Sure, you know what is right and what is wrong. But you also need someone to encourage you and to support your hard choices. Many young people do not have a family that will reassure them. No one may be around to tell them that they do not need drugs or alcohol to be cool or hip.

In the end, they make their own decisions—big decisions—that they really do not want to make alone. Emotionally, socially, and physically, they call the shots by themselves. Or they give in to peer pressure and let other people call the shots.

Drugs and alcohol can be hard to resist, especially if you think that you have to take them to have friends. If your family is not there for you, saying no is even harder.

CHAPTER 5

Is This Chemical Dependency?

*S*haneen *was coming home from a party one night, drunk and driving wildly. Pulling onto her street, she lost control of her friend's car and crashed into a telephone pole. She flew through the windshield. She smashed her mouth, knocked out several teeth, cut her face and arms, and suffered a severe concussion. The police told Shaneen that she was lucky to survive the crash.*

The accident terrified Shaneen. Her mother was furious and threatened to throw her out of the house. Shaneen thought of asking for help with her drinking problem, but she realized that her mother would not be able to help her. After all, her mother couldn't even help herself.

Shaneen had always told herself that she could handle her liquor. She wasn't hooked.

Some teens turn to alcohol as a way to forget the pain and loneliness they feel. However, it relieves the pain only temporarily.

She could stop anytime. Could she? she | **45**
wondered. Shaneen had never felt so alone.

Ray didn't know what to do. The fear of being without drugs, of being without money, and of dealing with everyday stresses, disappointments, and challenges had worn him to a frazzle.

Ray was using cocaine every day. He used as much as he could afford to buy. Many mornings it was hard for him to get out of bed. He couldn't function without a hit. The high lasted only a short time, and now he needed a lot more coke. The worst part was coming down. It left him exhausted, dazed, and weak.

Ray had lost all interest in his classes and his grades. He wasn't even sure if he was going to pass the year. But he didn't really care that much. All he cared about was the cocaine.

Shaneen and Ray are chemically dependent. Chemical dependency means that you have given up control of your life to chemical substances, such as cocaine and alcohol.

Do you need to have a car accident or total burnout to be chemically dependent? Not at all. Shaneen and Ray have been chemically dependent for a long time. Chemical dependency is part of a long process that started with taking that first drink or hit.

46 | *Two Types of Dependency*

There are two types of dependency: physical and psychological. Some drugs cause both. A physical dependency is when a person's body needs the drug and cannot function normally without it. The addict may show symptoms of withdrawal when he cannot take the drug. He may shake, sweat, become irritable, and in serious cases even hallucinate.

In a psychological addiction, the addict does not believe that he can live without the drug. He experiences a compulsive need to take the drug. Sometimes this craving occurs because the addict wants to feel the drug's pleasurable effects. In other cases the addict is afraid of suffering uncomfortable withdrawal symptoms.

When someone is chemically dependent, either physically or psychologically, he will do almost anything to get more of the drug.

Physical Addiction

Let's look at Shaneen's addiction. She now has to drink much more alcohol to experience the same high she once did. One beer used to give her a buzz, but now even a six-pack does not affect her. Shaneen's body has built up a level of tolerance to the drug's effects. As you learned earlier, tolerance is when you need more and more of a drug to get the same effect that you once got from smaller amounts.

Shaneen's body is physically dependent on alcohol. If Shaneen does not drink, she will have headaches, feel nauseated, experience shaking, and not be able to sleep. What does this mean? Her body requires alcohol in order to function, just as it requires bread and water.

Psychological Addiction

Ray, on the other hand, thinks he needs cocaine to feel normal. Without it, he is shy, quiet, and timid. But on coke, Ray feels as though everyone wants to be his friend. He is outgoing and confident. Ray does not believe that anyone will like him if he is his "old self." He needs cocaine to hang out with his friends, to meet girls, even to stay calm in front of his family. Ray cannot wait until his next hit.

What does this mean? He has a psychological dependency on cocaine. The drug controls his thinking and behavior. Even if his body does not need the drug, his mind is craving it. (And, remember, Ray is physically dependent, too.)

If you often feel depressed, and you use drugs or alcohol regularly, you may be chemically dependent.

Most alcoholics and drug addicts are both physically and psychologically dependent. The two often go hand in hand. For example, psychologically, Shaneen believes drinking makes her popular. Physically, Ray's body wants cocaine desperately. The two kinds of dependency are important to remember when you think about recovery. Remember, addiction is not as simple as it seems. Chemical dependency takes over your body and your mind.

Are You Chemically Dependent?
Here are some common indicators of chemical dependency:

- You need more and more of a drug to get the same high;

- You find you're willing to do **49** anything to get drugs, even things you know are wrong or illegal;
- You no longer take drugs for excitement, but to soothe your fears and pain;
- You take drugs to avoid painful withdrawal symptoms;
- You often feel depressed, as if the world has nothing to offer. You often think that you have no future;
- You cannot handle normal responsibilities, like school, work, or family duties;
- You often worry about finding money to buy more drugs or alcohol.

If you have answered "yes" to some of these questions, you might be developing a chemical dependency.

If you think you may be chemically dependent, talk to someone you trust about it. If you do not have someone you can confide in, you can call a drug abuse hotline and talk anonymously to a counselor. There are also many organizations that provide information and assistance for people battling chemical dependency. Some are listed in the back of this book.

CHAPTER 6

Finding a Way Out

*S*haneen didn't know to whom to turn for help. Her mother was never around, and when she was, all they did was argue. Her brother and sisters didn't want to talk to her about anything. Her father was too busy with his new family. No one had any time for Shaneen's problems.

The accident had made Shaneen realize that she had a problem with alcohol. She thought she might even be an alcoholic, like her mother.

There was one person Shaneen trusted a little. Her literature teacher was a young woman who seemed pretty cool. As a last resort, Shaneen went to see her after class. When Shaneen told her about her drinking problem, her teacher offered to look into treatment centers. She didn't seem shocked and didn't lecture Shaneen. Instead, she said she

was glad that Shaneen had told her. She said
that they could find help for Shaneen together.

Within a day, the teacher had located an inpatient program for alcoholics. Since it was an inpatient center, Shaneen could live there while she went through an intensive recovery treatment. The program was expensive, but there was financial assistance for people with low incomes. Shaneen agreed to go. She really wanted to get help, and she knew that there was no way to do that at home.

Ray woke up one morning feeling as if someone had been pounding him with a hammer all night. He couldn't get out of bed. It hurt just to move. He told his parents he was sick, and they let him stay home from school. They assumed he had the flu. When his brother came by, Ray knew that he wouldn't be able to fool him. His brother would know that it was cocaine that had done this to him.

Ray faced a moment of truth. He could say nothing and pretend he was sick. His brother wouldn't hassle him. Or he could ask for his brother's help. Ray decided that he needed to find a way out. He told his brother about his cocaine addiction. Surprisingly, his brother understood. He had seen a close friend go through a similar situation. For the first time in years, Ray felt as if he actually could communicate with someone

52 | *in his family. His brother offered to find a rehabilitation program for Ray and to help him tell their parents about the addiction.*

The Road to Recovery

The road to recovery is a difficult one. However, it does not have to be a lonely one. Remember, millions of people, including teens, have made the long journey back from chemical dependency to a healthy and happy life. If they can do it, so can you.

For a teen in a dysfunctional family, beating an addiction can be much harder than it is for people who have families to support them. You may feel as though you have nowhere to turn, or no one who cares about you. It may seem as if you have to not only beat your chemical dependency, but solve all of your family's problems, too.

This is not true. It may not be possible. Problems must be resolved one at a time. First, you have to solve your own problem—chemical dependency. After you become well, you may able to help your family become more functional. One thing you can always do is take care of yourself.

Choosing an Inpatient Program

An alcoholic or drug addict first must find immediate safety, as Shaneen did in the inpatient program. Shaneen needed a place where she could be physically and psychologically safe in order to recover. Her family's unstable and chaotic home would hurt her progress toward getting sober. She needed the stability of an inpatient treatment center, where she could live full-time during the recovery process. Here she could get the support, encouragement, care, and peace that she could not find at home.

Shaneen was not ready to confront her dysfunctional family's problems at first. And she learned that some families cannot be repaired. When that happens, you have to start building a support network of other people. Shaneen had to seek out relatives, friends, teachers, and other people who could give her stability, support, and love. The therapists at the treatment program taught her how to build a support network. When Shaneen was ready to leave, she also asked the staff for help in deciding her next step. She did not have to return home if she thought it would be bad for her.

Choosing an Outpatient Program

Unlike Shaneen, Ray did not feel threatened at home, just alone. With his brother's support, he was able to deal with his dependency at an outpatient treatment

If you want help recovering from chemical dependency, organizations that can assist you exist virtually everywhere.

center. At an outpatient program, Ray went to meetings and therapy during the day and returned home at night.

As part of his recovery process, Ray had to confront his family problems, too. He, his brother, and his parents attended family therapy together. They learned how to repair the damage in their dysfunctional family and how to become healthy again. Therapy taught Ray's family how to communicate openly, admit problems, and work together to solve them. It helped the family realize the behavior patterns that caused it to become dysfunctional.

Ray's family had a lot of work to do. Ray had to work on beating his chemical dependency. His brother had to learn to communicate with Ray. And their parents had to make their children a priority in their lives. All of them needed to trust one another again. Ray's family is very damaged, but with family therapy they have started to heal.

It's Your Choice

Your chemical dependency cannot be cured by someone else. No one else can save you. No one can force you to become clean. However, when you decide that you want help, there are people and organizations willing to help you. Inpatient and outpatient groups exist virtually everywhere. Support groups such as Alcoholics Anonymous, Cocaine Anonymous, and Narcotics Anonymous probably are located close to you. Schools, hospitals, religious organizations, and communities often have their own groups to help alcoholics and drug addicts recover. Many also have teen-only groups.

Through treatment, Shaneen and Ray were able to stop using drugs and alcohol. They began to deal with their chemical dependency, the problems it caused, and the pain and suffering it brought. In their rehab programs and in support groups, they learned about and met addicts who

Finding healthy and positive ways to deal with daily stress can help you beat chemical dependency.

had recovered from their addictions. They |
discussed what they wanted for their future, for their personal relationships, and for themselves. They talked about how to deal with old friends and offers for drugs and alcohol. They learned to resist peer pressure. They talked about rebuilding lives filled with new activities, new friends, and new plans.

Self-Help Groups

Shaneen and Ray also joined self-help groups, which were made up of teens struggling with drugs and alcohol. The self-help groups supported and encouraged them. They reminded Shaneen and Ray that many other teens were facing the same issues that they were. The groups gave them the strength to deal with old friends and old temptations. They also helped them to examine their families' dysfunction.

Most important, Shaneen and Ray realized that they had to begin new lives. They needed to deal with pain and confusion by means other than drugs and alcohol. Shaneen and Ray needed to find healthy and positive activities that would enhance their future, not drag them back into the misery of their past addiction. They were encouraged to consider activities and hobbies that they had not tried

58 | before. Shaneen wanted to work with young kids in the elementary school and to learn to paint. Ray started writing in a journal about his experience and wanted to start lessons in music or languages.

There is no easy way out for Shaneen or Ray. There never will be. Despite all of their family problems, they both have to take control of their own lives. They have to take charge of their addiction and of their recovery.

Ray and Shaneen have similar problems. However, they are from different families with different dysfunctions. Both are learning that some families can be repaired, but others cannot. In family therapy, Ray is working with his parents and his brother to make their home a more supportive and happier place. Shaneen, in contrast, might not be able to return to her family. She probably cannot make them functional again. However, Shaneen does not have to return to her old patterns of dysfunction—her drinking. She can learn more effective ways to cope with her family.

Shaneen and Ray are not responsible for repairing their families. They can take charge of only their own behavior. Now they have to face their chemical dependency and start healing themselves.

Glossary

addiction Chemical dependency.

chemical dependency To need drugs or alcohol compulsively and not be able to function without them, also called addiction.

codependency When someone ignores his or her own feelings in order to protect and care for someone else.

denial Refusal to admit the truth.

depressants Drugs, such as alcohol, that slow down your body and brain, also called downers.

downers Depressants.

drug abuse Using drugs or alcohol in a way that harms yourself and others while ignoring the hazardous consequences of your drug use.

dysfunctional Not working properly.

hallucinogens Drugs, such as marijuana, that cause hallucinations.

inhalants Drugs taken by inhaling.

inpatient treatment center A program that requires patients to live there during treatment and recovery.

60 **narcotics** Drugs, such as heroin, that dull the senses and reduce pain.

outpatient treatment center A daytime program that allows patients to return home in the evenings after treatment.

peer pressure When people your age try to convince you to do something you do not want to do.

physical dependency When your body cannot function normally without a drug.

psychological dependency When your mind desperately craves a drug.

recovery The process of getting well.

self-help program Teaches you how to help yourself by learning to improve yourself and resolve your problems.

stimulants Drugs, such as cocaine and amphetamines, that speed up your body and brain, also called uppers.

support group A set of people with a shared experience who give one another encouragement and guidance.

tolerance When you need more of a drug to get the same effect that you once got from smaller amounts.

uppers Stimulants.

withdrawal A painful syndrome that affects a drug addict's mind or body when he or she stops using drugs.

Where to Go for Help

Alcoholics Anonymous (AA)
P.O. Box 459
Grand Central Station
New York, NY 10163
(212) 870-3400
Web site: http.//www.
alcoholics-anonymous.
org

Children of Alcoholics Foundation
Box 4185
Grand Central Station
New York, NY 10163
(800) 488-3784

Narcotics Anonymous (NA)
World Service Office
19737 Nordhoff Place
Chatsworth, CA 91311
(818) 773-9999
e-mail: wso@aol.com

In Canada

Addictions Foundation of Manitoba
1031 Portage Avenue
Winnipeg, MB R3G 0R8
(204) 944-6200

Alcoholics Anonymous
Greater Toronto Area
Intergroup
234 Eglinton Avenue
East, Suite 202
Toronto, ON M4P 1K5
(416) 487-5591

61

For Further Reading

Jamiolkowski, Raymond. *Coping in a Dysfunctional Family*. Rev. ed. New York: The Rosen Publishing Group, 1998.

McFarland, Rhoda. *Coping with Substance Abuse*. Rev. ed. New York: The Rosen Publishing Group, 1990.

Rawls, Bea O'Donnell, and Gwen Johnson. *Drugs and Where to Turn*. New York: The Rosen Publishing Group, 1993.

Redes, Sharon. *Everything You Need to Know About Drug Abuse*. New York: The Rosen Publishing Group, 1998.

Seixas, Judith. *Drugs: What They Are, What They Do*. New York: Mulberry Books, 1991.

Yoder, Barbara. *The Recovery Resource Book*. New York: Fireside, 1990.

Index

About the Author

Jeff Biggers works as a freelance writer and consultant for adult literacy programs, as well as creative writing and literacy arts programs for at-risk youth. Mr. Biggers studied at Hunter College and Columbia University in New York City. He resides in Flagstaff, Arizona.

Photo Credits

pp. 2, 10, 14, 28, 44 by Lauren Piperno; p. 17 by Christine Innamorato; pp. 23, 48 by Ira Fox; p. 25 by Kim Sonsky/Matt Baumann; p. 32 by Michael Brandt; p. 39 by Les Mills; pp. 40, 56 by Ethan Zindler; p. 54 by Pablo Maldonado.